AROUND THE GLOBE

MUST SEE PLACES IN EUROPE

Speedy Publishing LLC

40 E. Main St. #1156

Newark, DE 19711

www.speedypublishing.com

Europe is a continent that comprises the westernmost peninsula of Eurasia. It is generally divided from Asia by the watershed divides of the Ural and Caucasus Mountains, the Ural River, the Caspian and Black Seas, and the Bosporus waterway connecting the Black and Aegean Seas. Europe is the world's second-smallest continent by surface area, covering about 10,180,000 square kilometres or 2% of the Earth's surface and about 6.8% of its land area.

AMSTERDAM

is the capital city and most populous city of the Kingdom of the Netherlands. Amsterdam's name derives from Amstelredamme, indicative of the city's origin as a dam of the river Amstel. There are 165 canals in Amsterdam. In total these waterways add up to more than 100 kilometers or about 60 miles.

AUSTRIA

is a federal republic and a landlocked country of over 8.5 million people in Central Europe. Austria is one of the richest countries in the world. The world's largest emerald (2860 carat) is displayed in the Imperial Treasury of the Hofburg (Imperial Palace) in Vienna. The oldest zoological garden in the world is the Tiergarten Schönbrunn in Vienna, founded in 1752.

ANFAHRT RECHTS

CZECH REPUBLIC

is a landlocked country in Central Europe bordered by Germany to the west, Austria to the south, Slovakia to the southeast and Poland to the northeast. The capital and largest city, Prague. The Czech Republic is almost entirely surrounded by mountains (except to the south, toward Austria and Slovakia). Mountains mark a natural border with Germany and Poland. Škoda Auto, one of the largest car manufacturers in Central Europe, is based in the Czech Republic. Czech people are the world's heaviest consumers of beer.

ENGLAND

is a country that is part of the United Kingdom. The name "England" is derived from the Old English name Englaland, which means "land of the Angles". The Angles were one of the Germanic tribes that settled in Great Britain during the Early Middle Ages. It is in England that the first postage stamps appeared.

FRANCE

is a unitary sovereign state comprising territory in western Europe and several overseas regions and territories. France is also know as 'the hexagon' because of its six-sided shape, France is sometimes referred to as l'hexagone. France is the world's most popular tourist destination, some 84.7 million visitors arrived in France, according to the World Tourism Organisation report published in 2014.

GERMANY

is a federal parliamentary republic in western-central Europe. Its capital and largest city is Berlin. Germany is the most populous member state in the European Union. After the United States, it is the second most popular migration destination in the world. Germany was the first country in the world to adopt Daylight saving time (DST), also known as summer time. This occured in 1916, in the midst of WWI. Berlin's Zoologischer Garten is the largest zoo in the world. Germany also boasts more than 400 registered zoos. Including zoological gardens, wildlife parks, aquariums, bird parks, animal reserves, or safari parkstotal, Germany has nearly 700 facilities.

GREECE

is a country located in southeastern Europe. Athens is the nation's capital and largest city, with Thessaloniki being the second largest and referred to as the co-capital. Greece has more archaeological museums than any other country in the world. Approximately 16.5 million tourists visit Greece each year, more than the country's entire population.

ICELAND

is a Nordic island country between the North Atlantic and the Arctic Ocean. Iceland is best known as the home of the first Viking explorers of North America, in the year 986. During the months of June and July, Iceland has days with a full 24 hours of precious, beautiful sunlight. The Northern Lights, also called Aurora Borealis, and Norðurljós in Icelandic, are one of the most spectacular shows on this earth and can frequently be seen in Iceland from September through March on clear and crisp nights.

IRELAND

is a sovereign state in north western Europe. The capital and largest city is Dublin, located in the eastern part of the island. The three most famous symbols of Ireland are the green Shamrock, the harp, and the Celtic cross. Ireland is a snake-free island. Due to its isolation from the European mainland, Ireland lacks several species common elsewhere in Europe, such as moles, weasels, polecats or roe deer. May is generally the driest month of the year in Ireland.

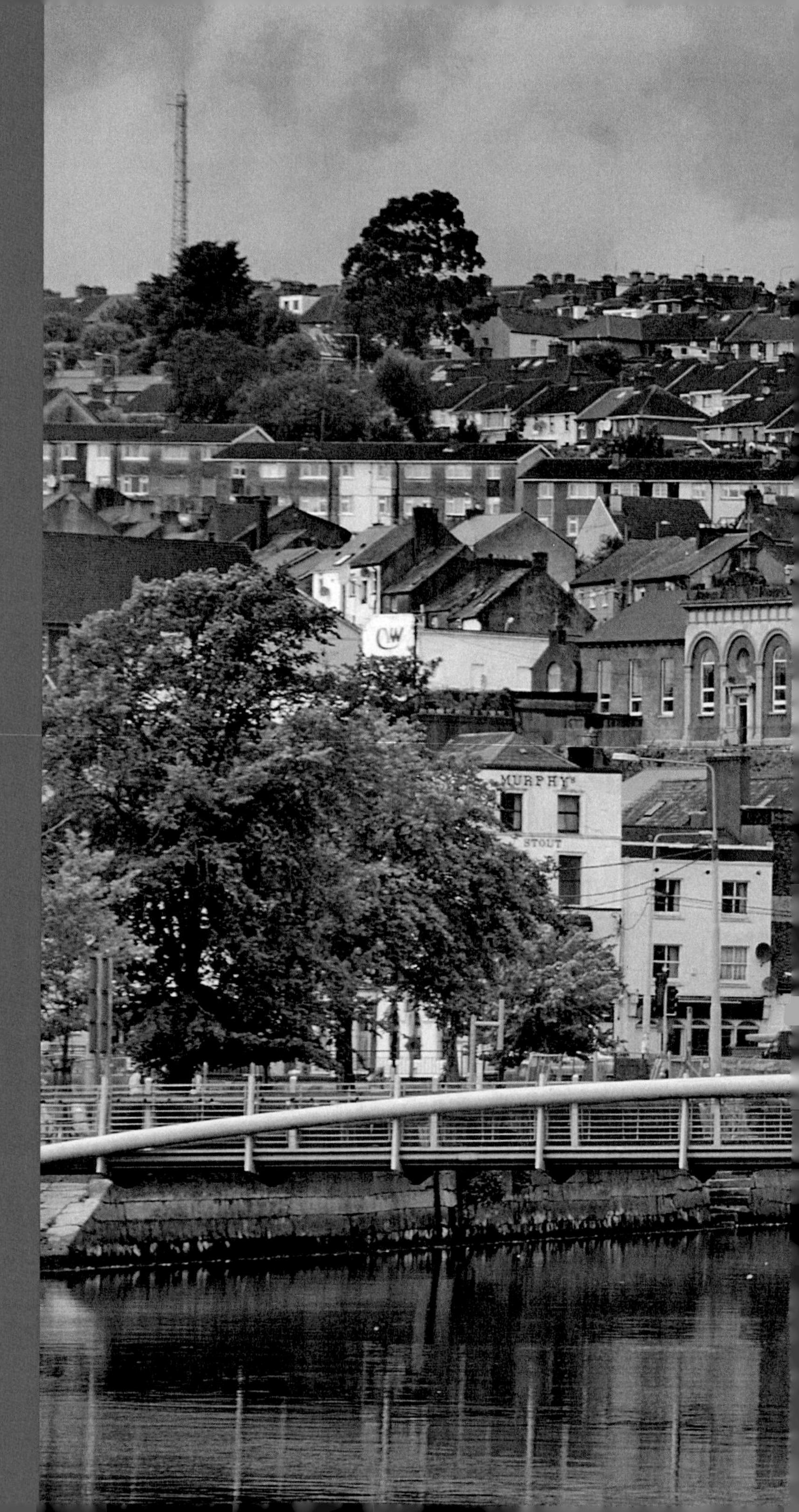

CLEMENS XII PONT MAX
AQVAM VIRGINEM
BENEDICTVS XIV

ITALY

is a unitary parliamentary republic in Southern Europe. Italy is regarded as one of the world's most industrialised nations and a leading country in world trade and exports. It is a highly developed country, with the world's 8th highest quality of life. The country is well known for its creative and innovative business, and for its influential and high-quality automobile, machinery, food, design and fashion industry. Many of the world's most prestigious sports cars are Italian, such as Ferrari, Lamborghini, Maserati, Bugatti or De Tomaso. Italy has more famous fashion designers than any other country, including Gucci, Prada, Versace, Dolce & Gabbana, Giorgio Armani, Ermenegildo Zegna, Gianfranco Ferré, Salvatore Ferragamo, Roberto Cavalli, Fendi, Valentino, Trussardi, Benetton.

RUSSIA

Russia is the largest country in the world, covering more than one-eighth of the Earth's inhabited land area. Russia is also the world's ninth most populous nation with nearly 144 million people as of 2015. Russia spans nine time zones and incorporates a wide range of environments and landforms. Russia has thousands of rivers and inland bodies of water, providing it with one of the world's largest surface water resources. Its lakes contain approximately one-quarter of the world's liquid fresh water. The largest and most prominent of Russia's bodies of fresh water is Lake Baikal, the world's deepest, purest, oldest and most capacious fresh water lake. aikal alone contains over one-fifth of the world's fresh surface water.

SCOTLAND

is a country that is part of the United Kingdom and covers the northern third of the island of Great Britain. The Bank of Scotland, founded in 1695, is the oldest surviving bank in the UK. It was also the first bank in Europe to print its own banknotes, a function it still performs today. The post office at Sanquhar, established in 1712, claims to be the oldest working post office in the world. The town also has the world's oldest curling society, formed in 1774 with sixty members.

SPAIN

is a sovereign state located on the Iberian Peninsula in southwestern Europe. By population, Spain is the sixth largest in Europe and the fifth in the European Union. The name Spain comes from the word Ispania, which means the land of rabbits. Spain is one of the world's leading countries in the development and production of renewable energy. In 2010 Spain became the solar power world leader when it overtook the United States with a massive power station plant called La Florida, near Alvarado, Badajoz.

SWEDEN

is a Scandinavian country in Northern Europe. Sweden is the third-largest country in the European Union by area. Sweden's parliament is called the Riksdag, to which members are elected every four years. Swedish women have their first child in average at 30 years old, the oldest in Europe along with Ireland and the Netherlands.

UKRAINE

is a country in Eastern Europe. The Ukraine currency is called the Hryvnia. Ukraine has long been a global breadbasket because of its extensive, fertile farmlands, and it remains one of the world's largest grain exporters. Ukrainian customs are heavily influenced by Christianity, the dominant religion in the country.

Made in the USA
Middletown, DE
02 December 2016